Mindfulness Journal for teens

© Copyright 2021 - All rights reserved.

You may not reproduce, duplicate or send the contents of this book without direct written permission from the author. You cannot hereby despite any circumstance blame the publisher or hold him or her to legal responsibility for any reparation, compensations, or monetary forfeiture owing to the information included herein, either in a direct or an indirect way.

Legal Notice: This book has copyright protection. You can use the book for personal purpose. You should not sell, use, alter, distribute, quote, take excerpts or paraphrase in part or whole the material contained in this book without obtaining the permission of the author first.

Disclaimer Notice: You must take note that the information in this document is for casual reading and entertainment purposes only.
We have made every attempt to provide accurate, up to date and reliable information. We do not express or imply guarantees of any kind. The persons who read admit that the writer is not occupied in giving legal, financial, medical or other advice. We put this book content by sourcing various places.

Please consult a licensed professional before you try any techniques shown in this book. By going through this document, the book lover comes to an agreement that under no situation is the author accountable for any forfeiture, direct or indirect, which they may incur because of the use of material contained in this document, including, but not limited to, — errors, omissions, or inaccuracies.

THIS JOURNAL BELONGS TO

MINDFULNESS DAILY JOURNAL

Date: ____/____/20__

Sun Mon Tue Wed Thu Fri Sat

IDEAS

MY MOOD TODAY

Today WILL BE A Good Day

Meditation

How long? ____/____   How was it? Hard ◯ Easy ◯

Excercise ◯   Yoga/Walking/Gym/Other _____

Today I Choose to Feel

_____
_____
_____

Today I Will Focus on

_____
_____
_____

Today I feel Inspired By

_____
_____
_____

Good Habits of The Day

_____
_____
_____

To Do List

- _____
- _____
- _____
- _____
- _____
- _____

Today I'm Grateful for

MINDFULNESS DAILY JOURNAL

MY DAY

10 MINUTES TO REFLECT ON YOUR DAY

3 Moments You'd Like To Remember

One Idea of Today That You'd Like To Explore Further

One of The Day's Challenges Big or Small

What I Did Wrong and How To Avoid That

MINDFULNESS DAILY JOURNAL

 **JOURNAL**

goal

MINDFULNESS DAILY JOURNAL

Date: ____/____/20__

Sun Mon Tue Wed Thu Fri Sat

IDEAS

MY MOOD TODAY

Today WILL BE A Good Day

Meditation

How long? ____/____

How was it? Hard ◯ Easy ◯

Excercise ◯   Yoga/Walking/Gym/Other _____

Today I Choose to Feel

_____
_____
_____

Today I Will Focus on

_____
_____
_____

Today I feel Inspired By

_____
_____
_____

Good Habits of The Day

_____
_____
_____

To Do List

☐ _____
☐ _____
☐ _____
☐ _____
☐ _____

Today I'm Grateful for

_____
_____
_____
_____
_____

MINDFULNESS DAILY JOURNAL

MY DAY

10 MINUTES TO REFLECT ON YOUR DAY

3 Moments You'd Like To Remember

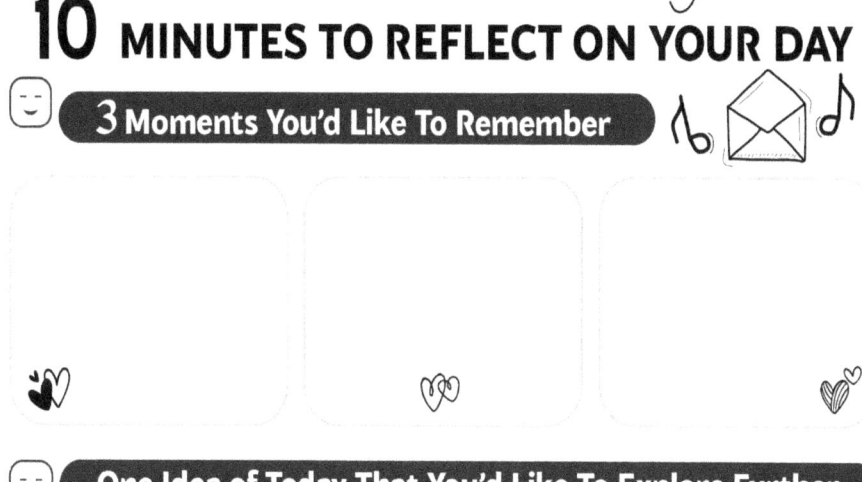

One Idea of Today That You'd Like To Explore Further

One of The Day's Challenges Big or Small

What I Did Wrong and How To Avoid That

MINDFULNESS DAILY JOURNAL

 **JOURNAL**

goal

MINDFULNESS DAILY JOURNAL

Date: ____/____/20__

Sun Mon Tue Wed Thu Fri Sat

IDEAS

MY MOOD TODAY

😊 🙁 😐 😄 😠

Today will be a Good Day

Meditation

How long? ____/____   How was it?   Hard ⬤   Easy ⬤

Excercise ⬤   Yoga/Walking/Gym/Other _____

Today I Choose to Feel
_____
_____
_____

Today I Will Focus on
_____
_____
_____

Today I feel Inspired By
_____
_____
_____

Good Habits of The Day
_____
_____
_____

To Do List
- _____
- _____
- _____
- _____
- _____
- _____

Today I'm Grateful for

MINDFULNESS DAILY JOURNAL

MY DAY

10 MINUTES TO REFLECT ON YOUR DAY

3 Moments You'd Like To Remember

One Idea of Today That You'd Like To Explore Further

One of The Day's Challenges Big or Small

What I Did Wrong and How To Avoid That

MINDFULNESS DAILY JOURNAL

 ## JOURNAL

goal

MINDFULNESS DAILY JOURNAL

Date: ____/____/20__

Sun ○ Mon ○ Tue ○ Wed ○ Thu ○ Fri ○ Sat ○

IDEAS

MY MOOD TODAY
😊 😖 😣 😄 😲

Today WILL BE A Good Day

Meditation

How long? ____/____   How was it?   Hard ○   Easy ○

Excercise ○   Yoga/Walking/Gym/Other _____

Today I Choose to Feel
_____
_____
_____

Today I Will Focus on
_____
_____
_____

Today I feel Inspired By
_____
_____
_____

Good Habits of The Day
_____
_____
_____

To Do List
○ _____
○ _____
○ _____
○ _____
○ _____

Today I'm Grateful for

MINDFULNESS DAILY JOURNAL

MY DAY

10 MINUTES TO REFLECT ON YOUR DAY

3 Moments You'd Like To Remember

One Idea of Today That You'd Like To Explore Further

One of The Day's Challenges Big or Small

What I Did Wrong and How To Avoid That

MINDFULNESS DAILY JOURNAL

 ## JOURNAL

goal

MINDFULNESS DAILY JOURNAL

Date: _____ / _____ /20__

Sun ○ Mon ○ Tue ○ Wed ○ Thu ○ Fri ○ Sat ○

MY MOOD TODAY

IDEAS   😊 ☹️ 😐 😄 😠   *Today Will Be A Good Day*

Meditation

How long? _____ / _____   How was it?   Hard ○   Easy ○

Excercise ○   Yoga/Walking/Gym/Other _____

Today I Choose to Feel
_____
_____
_____

Today I Will Focus on
_____
_____
_____

Today I feel Inspired By
_____
_____
_____

Good Habits of The Day
_____
_____
_____

To Do List
- _____
- _____
- _____
- _____
- _____
- _____

Today I'm Grateful for

MINDFULNESS DAILY JOURNAL

MY DAY

10 MINUTES TO REFLECT ON YOUR DAY

3 Moments You'd Like To Remember

One Idea of Today That You'd Like To Explore Further

One of The Day's Challenges Big or Small

What I Did Wrong and How To Avoid That

MINDFULNESS DAILY JOURNAL

JOURNAL

goal

MINDFULNESS DAILY JOURNAL

Date: ____/____/20__

Sun ○ Mon ○ Tue ○ Wed ○ Thu ○ Fri ○ Sat ○

IDEAS

MY MOOD TODAY

Today Will Be A Good Day

Meditation

How long? ____/____

How was it? Hard ○ Easy ○

Excercise ○

Yoga/Walking/Gym/Other _____

Today I Choose to Feel

_____
_____
_____

Today I Will Focus on

_____
_____
_____

Today I feel Inspired By

_____
_____
_____

Good Habits of The Day

_____
_____
_____

To Do List

○ _____
○ _____
○ _____
○ _____
○ _____

Today I'm Grateful for

MINDFULNESS DAILY JOURNAL

MY DAY

10 MINUTES TO REFLECT ON YOUR DAY

3 Moments You'd Like To Remember

One Idea of Today That You'd Like To Explore Further

One of The Day's Challenges Big or Small

What I Did Wrong and How To Avoid That

MINDFULNESS DAILY JOURNAL

 **JOURNAL**

goal

MINDFULNESS DAILY JOURNAL

Date: ____ / ____ /20__

Sun Mon Tue Wed Thu Fri Sat

IDEAS

MY MOOD TODAY

Today WILL BE A Good Day

Meditation

How long? ____ / ____   How was it? Hard ⬯ Easy ⬯

Excercise ⬯   Yoga/Walking/Gym/Other _____

Today I Choose to Feel

_____
_____
_____

Today I Will Focus on

_____
_____
_____

Today I feel Inspired By

_____
_____
_____

Good Habits of The Day

_____
_____
_____

To Do List

- _____
- _____
- _____
- _____
- _____

Today I'm Grateful for

_____
_____
_____

MINDFULNESS DAILY JOURNAL

MY DAY

10 MINUTES TO REFLECT ON YOUR DAY

3 Moments You'd Like To Remember

One Idea of Today That You'd Like To Explore Further

One of The Day's Challenges Big or Small

What I Did Wrong and How To Avoid That

MINDFULNESS DAILY JOURNAL

 ## JOURNAL

goal

MINDFULNESS DAILY JOURNAL

Date: _____/_____/20___

Sun ◯ Mon ◯ Tue ◯ Wed ◯ Thu ◯ Fri ◯ Sat ◯

IDEAS

MY MOOD TODAY
😊 ☹️ 😦 😄 😠

Today Will Be A Good Day

Meditation

How long? _____/_____   How was it? Hard ◯ Easy ◯

Exercise ◯   Yoga/Walking/Gym/Other _____

Today I Choose to Feel
_____
_____
_____

Today I Will Focus on
_____
_____
_____

Today I feel Inspired By
_____
_____
_____

Good Habits of The Day
_____
_____
_____

To Do List
◯ _____
◯ _____
◯ _____
◯ _____
◯ _____

Today I'm Grateful for
_____
_____
_____
_____
_____

MINDFULNESS DAILY JOURNAL

MY DAY

10 MINUTES TO REFLECT ON YOUR DAY

3 Moments You'd Like To Remember

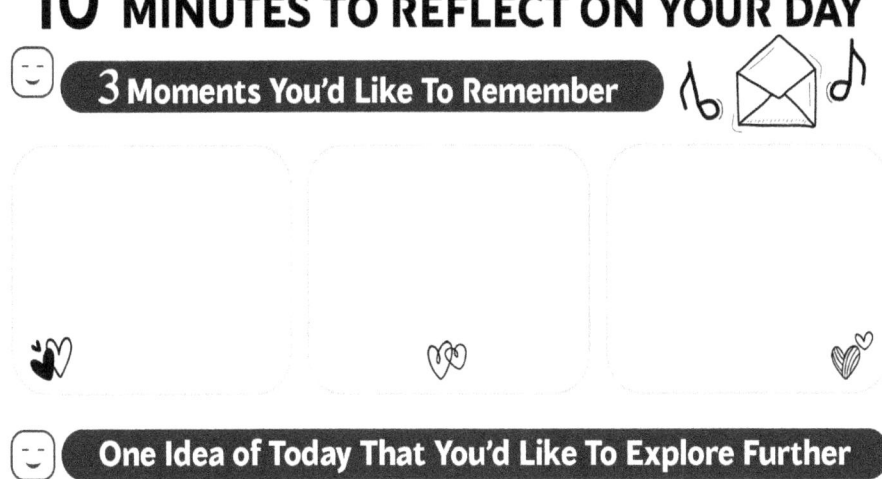

One Idea of Today That You'd Like To Explore Further

One of The Day's Challenges Big or Small

What I Did Wrong and How To Avoid That

MINDFULNESS DAILY JOURNAL

 ## JOURNAL

goal

MINDFULNESS DAILY JOURNAL

Date: ____/____/20__

Sun ○ Mon ○ Tue ○ Wed ○ Thu ○ Fri ○ Sat ○

IDEAS

MY MOOD TODAY

😊 😞 😐 😄 😠

Today WILL BE A Good Day

Meditation

How long? ____/____   How was it? Hard ○ Easy ○

Excercise ○   Yoga/Walking/Gym/Other _____

Today I Choose to Feel
_____
_____
_____

Today I Will Focus on
_____
_____
_____

Today I feel Inspired By
_____
_____
_____

Good Habits of The Day
_____
_____
_____

To Do List
○ _____
○ _____
○ _____
○ _____
○ _____
○ _____

Today I'm Grateful for
_____
_____
_____
_____

MINDFULNESS DAILY JOURNAL

MY DAY

10 MINUTES TO REFLECT ON YOUR DAY

3 Moments You'd Like To Remember

One Idea of Today That You'd Like To Explore Further

One of The Day's Challenges Big or Small

What I Did Wrong and How To Avoid That

MINDFULNESS DAILY JOURNAL

 ## JOURNAL

goal

MINDFULNESS DAILY JOURNAL

Date: ____/____/20__

Sun   Mon   Tue   Wed   Thu   Fri   Sat

IDEAS

MY MOOD TODAY

Today WILL BE A Good Day

Meditation

How long? ____/____   How was it?   Hard ◯   Easy ◯

Excercise ◯   Yoga/Walking/Gym/Other _____

Today I Choose to Feel

_____
_____
_____

Today I Will Focus on

_____
_____
_____

Today I feel Inspired By

_____
_____
_____

Good Habits of The Day

_____
_____
_____

To Do List

☐ _____
☐ _____
☐ _____
☐ _____
☐ _____

Today I'm Grateful for

MINDFULNESS DAILY JOURNAL

MY DAY

10 MINUTES TO REFLECT ON YOUR DAY

3 Moments You'd Like To Remember

One Idea of Today That You'd Like To Explore Further

One of The Day's Challenges Big or Small

What I Did Wrong and How To Avoid That

MINDFULNESS DAILY JOURNAL

 ## JOURNAL

goal

MINDFULNESS DAILY JOURNAL

Date: ____/____/20__

Sun ○ Mon ○ Tue ○ Wed ○ Thu ○ Fri ○ Sat ○

IDEAS

MY MOOD TODAY
😊 🙁 😐 😄 😠

Today Will Be A Good Day

Meditation

How long? ____/____   How was it?   Hard ○   Easy ○

Excercise ○   Yoga/Walking/Gym/Other _____

Today I Choose to Feel
_____
_____
_____

Today I Will Focus on
_____
_____
_____

Today I feel Inspired By
_____
_____
_____

Good Habits of The Day
_____
_____
_____

To Do List
○ _____
○ _____
○ _____
○ _____
○ _____
○ _____

Today I'm Grateful for

MINDFULNESS DAILY JOURNAL

MY DAY

10 MINUTES TO REFLECT ON YOUR DAY

3 Moments You'd Like To Remember

One Idea of Today That You'd Like To Explore Further

One of The Day's Challenges Big or Small

What I Did Wrong and How To Avoid That

MINDFULNESS DAILY JOURNAL

 **JOURNAL**

goal

MINDFULNESS DAILY JOURNAL

Date: ____/____/20__

Sun ○ Mon ○ Tue ○ Wed ○ Thu ○ Fri ○ Sat ○

IDEAS

MY MOOD TODAY
😊 ☹️ 😣 😄 😲

Today WILL BE A Good Day

Meditation

How long? ____ /____   How was it? Hard ○ Easy ○

Excercise ○   Yoga/Walking/Gym/Other _____

Today I Choose to Feel
_____
_____
_____

Today I Will Focus on
_____
_____
_____

Today I feel Inspired By
_____
_____
_____

Good Habits of The Day
_____
_____
_____

To Do List
☐ _____
☐ _____
☐ _____
☐ _____
☐ _____

Today I'm Grateful for
_____
_____
_____
_____

MINDFULNESS DAILY JOURNAL

MY DAY

10 MINUTES TO REFLECT ON YOUR DAY

3 Moments You'd Like To Remember

One Idea of Today That You'd Like To Explore Further

One of The Day's Challenges Big or Small

What I Did Wrong and How To Avoid That

MINDFULNESS DAILY JOURNAL

 JOURNAL

goal

MINDFULNESS DAILY JOURNAL

Date: ____/____/20__

Sun ○ Mon ○ Tue ○ Wed ○ Thu ○ Fri ○ Sat ○

IDEAS

MY MOOD TODAY

Today WILL BE A Good Day

Meditation

How long? ____/____   How was it? Hard ○   Easy ○

Excercise ○   Yoga/Walking/Gym/Other _____

Today I Choose to Feel
_____
_____
_____

Today I Will Focus on
_____
_____
_____

Today I feel Inspired By
_____
_____
_____

Good Habits of The Day
_____
_____
_____

To Do List
- _____
- _____
- _____
- _____
- _____
- _____

Today I'm Grateful for

MINDFULNESS DAILY JOURNAL

MY DAY

10 MINUTES TO REFLECT ON YOUR DAY

3 Moments You'd Like To Remember

One Idea of Today That You'd Like To Explore Further

One of The Day's Challenges Big or Small

What I Did Wrong and How To Avoid That

MINDFULNESS DAILY JOURNAL

 ## JOURNAL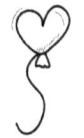

goal

MINDFULNESS DAILY JOURNAL

Date: ____/____/20__

Sun ○ Mon ○ Tue ○ Wed ○ Thu ○ Fri ○ Sat ○

IDEAS

MY MOOD TODAY 😊 😕 ☹️ 😀 😲

Today Will Be A Good Day

Meditation

How long? ____/____

How was it?   Hard ○   Easy ○

Excercise ○   Yoga/Walking/Gym/Other _____

Today I Choose to Feel
_____
_____
_____

Today I Will Focus on
_____
_____
_____

Today I feel Inspired By
_____
_____
_____

Good Habits of The Day
_____
_____
_____

To Do List
○ _____
○ _____
○ _____
○ _____
○ _____

Today I'm Grateful for

MINDFULNESS DAILY JOURNAL

MY DAY

10 MINUTES TO REFLECT ON YOUR DAY

3 Moments You'd Like To Remember

One Idea of Today That You'd Like To Explore Further

One of The Day's Challenges Big or Small

What I Did Wrong and How To Avoid That

MINDFULNESS DAILY JOURNAL

 ## JOURNAL

goal

MINDFULNESS DAILY JOURNAL

Date: ____/____/20__

Sun ○ Mon ● Tue ○ Wed ○ Thu ● Fri ○ Sat ○

IDEAS

MY MOOD TODAY
😊 ☹️ 😣 😄 😠

Today will be a Good Day

Meditation

How long? ____/____   How was it? Hard ○ Easy ○

Excercise ○   Yoga/Walking/Gym/Other _____

Today I Choose to Feel
_____
_____
_____

Today I Will Focus on
_____
_____
_____

Today I feel Inspired By
_____
_____
_____

Good Habits of The Day
_____
_____
_____

To Do List
- _____
- _____
- _____
- _____
- _____

Today I'm Grateful for

MINDFULNESS DAILY JOURNAL

MY DAY

10 MINUTES TO REFLECT ON YOUR DAY

3 Moments You'd Like To Remember

One Idea of Today That You'd Like To Explore Further

One of The Day's Challenges Big or Small

What I Did Wrong and How To Avoid That

MINDFULNESS DAILY JOURNAL

JOURNAL

goal

MINDFULNESS DAILY JOURNAL

Date: ____/____/20__

Sun Mon Tue Wed Thu Fri Sat

IDEAS

MY MOOD TODAY

Today WILL BE A Good Day

Meditation

How long? ____/____

How was it? Hard ◯ Easy ◯

Excercise ◯   Yoga/Walking/Gym/Other _____

Today I Choose to Feel

_____
_____
_____

Today I Will Focus on

_____
_____
_____

Today I feel Inspired By

_____
_____
_____

Good Habits of The Day

_____
_____
_____

To Do List

☐ _____
☐ _____
☐ _____
☐ _____
☐ _____

Today I'm Grateful for

MINDFULNESS DAILY JOURNAL

MY DAY

10 MINUTES TO REFLECT ON YOUR DAY

3 Moments You'd Like To Remember

One Idea of Today That You'd Like To Explore Further

One of The Day's Challenges Big or Small

What I Did Wrong and How To Avoid That

MINDFULNESS DAILY JOURNAL

 JOURNAL

goal

MINDFULNESS DAILY JOURNAL

Date: ____/____/20__

Sun Mon Tue Wed Thu Fri Sat

IDEAS

MY MOOD TODAY

Today WILL BE A Good Day

Meditation

How long? ____/____   How was it?   Hard ◯   Easy ◯

Excercise ◯   Yoga/Walking/Gym/Other _____

Today I Choose to Feel

_____
_____
_____

Today I Will Focus on

_____
_____
_____

Today I feel Inspired By

_____
_____
_____

Good Habits of The Day

_____
_____
_____

To Do List

- _____
- _____
- _____
- _____
- _____
- _____

Today I'm Grateful for

MINDFULNESS DAILY JOURNAL

MY DAY

10 MINUTES TO REFLECT ON YOUR DAY

3 Moments You'd Like To Remember

One Idea of Today That You'd Like To Explore Further

One of The Day's Challenges Big or Small

What I Did Wrong and How To Avoid That

MINDFULNESS DAILY JOURNAL

 ## JOURNAL

goal

MINDFULNESS DAILY JOURNAL

Date: ____/____/20__

Sun Mon Tue Wed Thu Fri Sat

IDEAS

MY MOOD TODAY

Today WILL BE A Good Day

Meditation

How long? ____/____   How was it? Hard ◯ Easy ◯

Excercise ◯   Yoga/Walking/Gym/Other _____

Today I Choose to Feel

Today I Will Focus on

Today I feel Inspired By

Good Habits of The Day

To Do List

Today I'm Grateful for

MINDFULNESS DAILY JOURNAL

MY DAY

10 MINUTES TO REFLECT ON YOUR DAY

3 Moments You'd Like To Remember

One Idea of Today That You'd Like To Explore Further

One of The Day's Challenges Big or Small

What I Did Wrong and How To Avoid That

MINDFULNESS DAILY JOURNAL

 ## JOURNAL

goal

MINDFULNESS DAILY JOURNAL

Date: _____/_____/20___

Sun ○ Mon ○ Tue ○ Wed ○ Thu ○ Fri ○ Sat ○

IDEAS

MY MOOD TODAY ☺ ☹ 😠 😄 😮

Today WILL BE A Good Day

Meditation

How long? _____/_____   How was it?   Hard ○   Easy ○

Excercise ○   Yoga/Walking/Gym/Other _____

Today I Choose to Feel
_____
_____
_____

Today I Will Focus on
_____
_____
_____

Today I feel Inspired By
_____
_____
_____

Good Habits of The Day
_____
_____
_____

To Do List
○ _____
○ _____
○ _____
○ _____
○ _____

Today I'm Grateful for
_____
_____
_____
_____
_____

MINDFULNESS DAILY JOURNAL

MY DAY

10 MINUTES TO REFLECT ON YOUR DAY

3 Moments You'd Like To Remember

One Idea of Today That You'd Like To Explore Further

One of The Day's Challenges Big or Small

What I Did Wrong and How To Avoid That

MINDFULNESS DAILY JOURNAL

JOURNAL

goal

MINDFULNESS DAILY JOURNAL

Date: ___/___/20__

Sun Mon Tue Wed Thu Fri Sat

IDEAS

MY MOOD TODAY

Today Will Be A Good Day

Meditation

How long? ___/___

How was it? Hard ○ Easy ○

Excercise ○   Yoga/Walking/Gym/Other _____

Today I Choose to Feel

Today I Will Focus on

Today I feel Inspired By

Good Habits of The Day

To Do List

Today I'm Grateful for

MINDFULNESS DAILY JOURNAL

MY DAY

10 MINUTES TO REFLECT ON YOUR DAY

3 Moments You'd Like To Remember

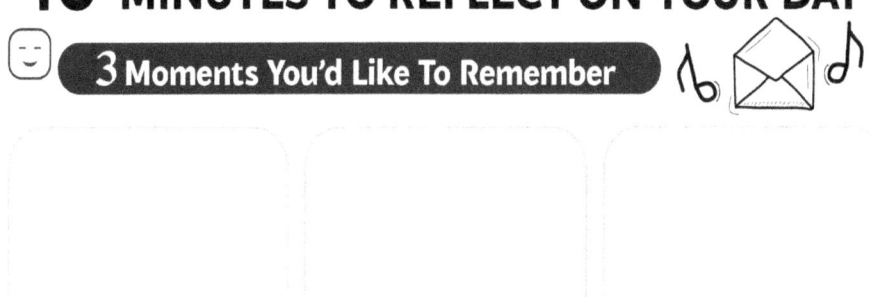

One Idea of Today That You'd Like To Explore Further

One of The Day's Challenges Big or Small

What I Did Wrong and How To Avoid That

MINDFULNESS DAILY JOURNAL

 JOURNAL

goal

MINDFULNESS DAILY JOURNAL

Date: ____ / ____ /20__

Sun   Mon   Tue   Wed   Thu   Fri   Sat

IDEAS

MY MOOD TODAY

Today Will Be A Good Day

Meditation

How long? ____ / ____   How was it?   Hard ◯   Easy ◯

Excercise ◯   Yoga/Walking/Gym/Other _____

Today I Choose to Feel

_____
_____
_____

Today I Will Focus on

_____
_____
_____

Today I feel Inspired By

_____
_____
_____

Good Habits of The Day

_____
_____
_____

To Do List

- _____
- _____
- _____
- _____
- _____
- _____

Today I'm Grateful for

_____
_____
_____
_____

MINDFULNESS DAILY JOURNAL

MY DAY

10 MINUTES TO REFLECT ON YOUR DAY

3 Moments You'd Like To Remember

One Idea of Today That You'd Like To Explore Further

One of The Day's Challenges Big or Small

What I Did Wrong and How To Avoid That

MINDFULNESS DAILY JOURNAL

JOURNAL

goal

MINDFULNESS DAILY JOURNAL

Date: ____/____/20__

Sun ◯ Mon ◯ Tue ◯ Wed ◯ Thu ◯ Fri ◯ Sat ◯

IDEAS

MY MOOD TODAY

Today WILL BE A Good Day

Meditation

How long? ____/____

How was it? Hard ◯ Easy ◯

Excercise ◯   Yoga/Walking/Gym/Other _____

Today I Choose to Feel
_____
_____
_____

Today I Will Focus on
_____
_____
_____

Today I feel Inspired By
_____
_____
_____

Good Habits of The Day
_____
_____
_____

To Do List
☐ _____
☐ _____
☐ _____
☐ _____
☐ _____

Today I'm Grateful for
_____
_____
_____
_____
_____

MINDFULNESS DAILY JOURNAL

MY DAY

10 MINUTES TO REFLECT ON YOUR DAY

3 Moments You'd Like To Remember

One Idea of Today That You'd Like To Explore Further

One of The Day's Challenges Big or Small

What I Did Wrong and How To Avoid That

MINDFULNESS DAILY JOURNAL

 ## JOURNAL

goal

MINDFULNESS DAILY JOURNAL

Date: ____/____/20__

Sun ○ Mon ○ Tue ○ Wed ○ Thu ○ Fri ○ Sat ○

IDEAS

MY MOOD TODAY 😊 ☹️ 😐 😄 😠

Today WILL BE A Good Day

Meditation

How long? ____/____   How was it? Hard ○ Easy ○

Excercise ○   Yoga/Walking/Gym/Other _____

Today I Choose to Feel

_____
_____
_____

Today I Will Focus on

_____
_____
_____

Today I feel Inspired By

_____
_____
_____

Good Habits of The Day

_____
_____
_____

To Do List

○ _____
○ _____
○ _____
○ _____
○ _____
○ _____

Today I'm Grateful for

MINDFULNESS DAILY JOURNAL

MY DAY

10 MINUTES TO REFLECT ON YOUR DAY

3 Moments You'd Like To Remember

One Idea of Today That You'd Like To Explore Further

One of The Day's Challenges Big or Small

What I Did Wrong and How To Avoid That

MINDFULNESS DAILY JOURNAL

JOURNAL

goal

MINDFULNESS DAILY JOURNAL

Date: ____/____/20__

Sun ○ Mon ○ Tue ○ Wed ○ Thu ○ Fri ○ Sat ○

IDEAS

MY MOOD TODAY
😊 😟 😢 😄 😠

Today Will Be A Good Day

Meditation

How long? ____/____

How was it? Hard ○ Easy ○

Excercise ○   Yoga/Walking/Gym/Other _____

Today I Choose to Feel
_____
_____
_____

Today I Will Focus on
_____
_____
_____

Today I feel Inspired By
_____
_____
_____

Good Habits of The Day
_____
_____
_____

To Do List
- _____
- _____
- _____
- _____
- _____

Today I'm Grateful for

MINDFULNESS DAILY JOURNAL

Date: ____/____/20__

Sun Mon Tue Wed Thu Fri Sat

IDEAS

MY MOOD TODAY

Today Will Be A Good Day

Meditation

How long? ____/____   How was it?   Hard ◯   Easy ◯

Exercise ◯   Yoga/Walking/Gym/Other _____

Today I Choose to Feel

_____
_____
_____

Today I Will Focus on

_____
_____
_____

Today I feel Inspired By

_____
_____
_____

Good Habits of The Day

_____
_____
_____

To Do List

☐ _____
☐ _____
☐ _____
☐ _____
☐ _____

Today I'm Grateful for

MINDFULNESS DAILY JOURNAL

MY DAY

10 MINUTES TO REFLECT ON YOUR DAY

3 Moments You'd Like To Remember

One Idea of Today That You'd Like To Explore Further

One of The Day's Challenges Big or Small

What I Did Wrong and How To Avoid That

MINDFULNESS DAILY JOURNAL

 ## JOURNAL

goal

MINDFULNESS DAILY JOURNAL

Date: ____ /____ /20__

Sun Mon Tue Wed Thu Fri Sat

IDEAS

MY MOOD TODAY

Today Will Be A Good Day

Meditation

How long? ____ /____

How was it? Hard ◯ Easy ◯

Excercise ◯   Yoga/Walking/Gym/Other _____

Today I Choose to Feel

_____
_____
_____

Today I Will Focus on

_____
_____
_____

Today I feel Inspired By

_____
_____
_____

Good Habits of The Day

_____
_____
_____

To Do List

- _____
- _____
- _____
- _____
- _____

Today I'm Grateful for

MINDFULNESS DAILY JOURNAL

MY DAY

10 MINUTES TO REFLECT ON YOUR DAY

3 Moments You'd Like To Remember

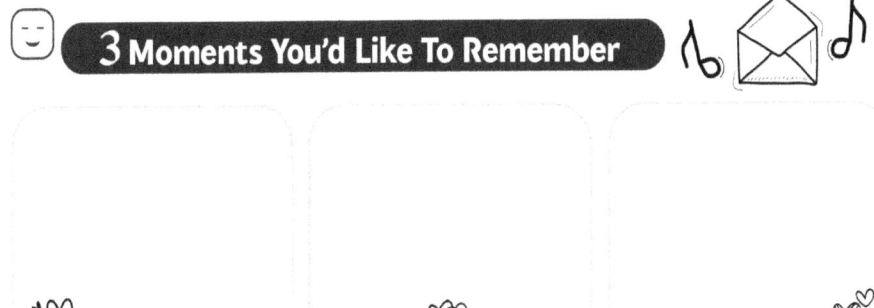

One Idea of Today That You'd Like To Explore Further

One of The Day's Challenges Big or Small

What I Did Wrong and How To Avoid That

MINDFULNESS DAILY JOURNAL

 **JOURNAL**

goal

MINDFULNESS DAILY JOURNAL

Date: ____/____/20__

Sun ○ Mon ○ Tue ○ Wed ○ Thu ○ Fri ○ Sat ○

IDEAS

MY MOOD TODAY

Today WILL BE A Good Day

Meditation

How long? ____/____   How was it? Hard ○   Easy ○

Excercise ○   Yoga/Walking/Gym/Other _____

Today I Choose to Feel

_____
_____
_____

Today I Will Focus on

_____
_____
_____

Today I feel Inspired By

_____
_____
_____

Good Habits of The Day

_____
_____
_____

To Do List

○ _____
○ _____
○ _____
○ _____
○ _____

Today I'm Grateful for

_____
_____
_____
_____
_____

MINDFULNESS DAILY JOURNAL

MY DAY

10 MINUTES TO REFLECT ON YOUR DAY

3 Moments You'd Like To Remember

One Idea of Today That You'd Like To Explore Further

One of The Day's Challenges Big or Small

What I Did Wrong and How To Avoid That

MINDFULNESS DAILY JOURNAL

 **JOURNAL**

goal

MINDFULNESS DAILY JOURNAL

Date: ____/____/20__

Sun ◯ Mon ◯ Tue ◯ Wed ◯ Thu ◯ Fri ◯ Sat ◯

IDEAS

MY MOOD TODAY
☺ ☹ 😟 😄 😠

Today WILL BE A Good Day

Meditation

How long? ____/____

How was it?   Hard ◯   Easy ◯

Excercise ◯   Yoga/Walking/Gym/Other _____

Today I Choose to Feel
_____
_____
_____

Today I Will Focus on
_____
_____
_____

Today I feel Inspired By
_____
_____
_____

Good Habits of The Day
_____
_____
_____

To Do List
◯ _____
◯ _____
◯ _____
◯ _____
◯ _____

Today I'm Grateful for

MINDFULNESS DAILY JOURNAL

MY DAY

10 MINUTES TO REFLECT ON YOUR DAY

3 Moments You'd Like To Remember

One Idea of Today That You'd Like To Explore Further

One of The Day's Challenges Big or Small

What I Did Wrong and How To Avoid That

MINDFULNESS DAILY JOURNAL

 ## JOURNAL

goal

MINDFULNESS DAILY JOURNAL

Date: _____/_____/20__

Sun ○ Mon ○ Tue ○ Wed ○ Thu ○ Fri ○ Sat ○

IDEAS

MY MOOD TODAY
☺ ☹ 😐 😄 😠

Today will be a Good Day

Meditation

How long? _____/_____   How was it? Hard ○   Easy ○

Excercise ○   Yoga/Walking/Gym/Other _____

Today I Choose to Feel
_____
_____
_____

Today I Will Focus on
_____
_____
_____

Today I feel Inspired By
_____
_____
_____

Good Habits of The Day
_____
_____
_____

To Do List
☐ _____
☐ _____
☐ _____
☐ _____
☐ _____

Today I'm Grateful for
_____
_____
_____
_____
_____

MINDFULNESS DAILY JOURNAL

MY DAY

10 MINUTES TO REFLECT ON YOUR DAY

3 Moments You'd Like To Remember

One Idea of Today That You'd Like To Explore Further

One of The Day's Challenges Big or Small

What I Did Wrong and How To Avoid That

MINDFULNESS DAILY JOURNAL

JOURNAL

goal

MINDFULNESS DAILY JOURNAL

Date: ____/____/20__

Sun ○ Mon ○ Tue ○ Wed ○ Thu ○ Fri ○ Sat ○

IDEAS

MY MOOD TODAY

😊 😕 ☹ 😃 😠

Today will be a Good Day

Meditation

How long? ____/____

How was it? Hard ○ Easy ○

Excercise ○   Yoga/Walking/Gym/Other _____

Today I Choose to Feel

_____
_____
_____

Today I Will Focus on

_____
_____
_____

Today I feel Inspired By

_____
_____
_____

Good Habits of The Day

_____
_____
_____

To Do List

○ _____
○ _____
○ _____
○ _____
○ _____

Today I'm Grateful for

MINDFULNESS DAILY JOURNAL

MY DAY

10 MINUTES TO REFLECT ON YOUR DAY

3 Moments You'd Like To Remember

One Idea of Today That You'd Like To Explore Further

One of The Day's Challenges Big or Small

What I Did Wrong and How To Avoid That

MINDFULNESS DAILY JOURNAL

 **JOURNAL**

goal

MINDFULNESS DAILY JOURNAL

Date: ____/____/20__

Sun ◯ Mon ◯ Tue ◯ Wed ◯ Thu ◯ Fri ◯ Sat ◯

IDEAS

MY MOOD TODAY
😊 ☹️ 😕 😄 😠

Today Will Be A Good Day

Meditation

How long? ____/____   How was it?   Hard ◯   Easy ◯

Excercise ◯   Yoga/Walking/Gym/Other _____

Today I Choose to Feel
_____
_____
_____

Today I Will Focus on
_____
_____
_____

Today I feel Inspired By
_____
_____
_____

Good Habits of The Day
_____
_____
_____

To Do List
◯ _____
◯ _____
◯ _____
◯ _____
◯ _____
◯ _____

Today I'm Grateful for

MINDFULNESS DAILY JOURNAL

MY DAY

10 MINUTES TO REFLECT ON YOUR DAY

3 Moments You'd Like To Remember

One Idea of Today That You'd Like To Explore Further

One of The Day's Challenges Big or Small

What I Did Wrong and How To Avoid That

MINDFULNESS DAILY JOURNAL

JOURNAL

goal

MINDFULNESS DAILY JOURNAL

Date: ____/____/20__

Sun Mon Tue Wed Thu Fri Sat

IDEAS

MY MOOD TODAY

Today WILL BE A Good Day

Meditation

How long? ____/____

How was it? Hard ◯ Easy ◯

Excercise ◯   Yoga/Walking/Gym/Other _____

Today I Choose to Feel

_____
_____
_____

Today I Will Focus on

_____
_____
_____

Today I feel Inspired By

_____
_____
_____

Good Habits of The Day

_____
_____
_____

To Do List

◯ _____
◯ _____
◯ _____
◯ _____
◯ _____

Today I'm Grateful for

MINDFULNESS DAILY JOURNAL

MY DAY

10 MINUTES TO REFLECT ON YOUR DAY

3 Moments You'd Like To Remember

One Idea of Today That You'd Like To Explore Further

One of The Day's Challenges Big or Small

What I Did Wrong and How To Avoid That

MINDFULNESS DAILY JOURNAL

 ## JOURNAL

goal

MINDFULNESS DAILY JOURNAL

Date: ____/____/20__

Sun Mon Tue Wed Thu Fri Sat

IDEAS

MY MOOD TODAY

Today WILL BE A Good Day

Meditation

How long? ____/____   How was it?   Hard ◯   Easy ◯

Excercise ◯   Yoga/Walking/Gym/Other _____

Today I Choose to Feel

_____
_____
_____

Today I Will Focus on

_____
_____
_____

Today I feel Inspired By

_____
_____
_____

Good Habits of The Day

_____
_____
_____

To Do List

- _____
- _____
- _____
- _____
- _____
- _____

Today I'm Grateful for

MINDFULNESS DAILY JOURNAL

MY DAY

10 MINUTES TO REFLECT ON YOUR DAY

3 Moments You'd Like To Remember

One Idea of Today That You'd Like To Explore Further

One of The Day's Challenges Big or Small

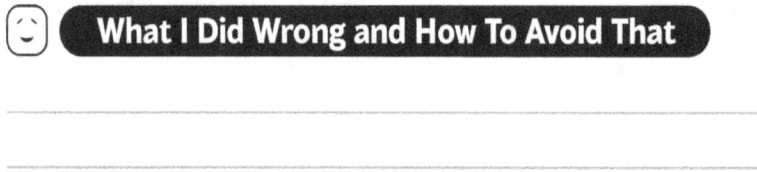

What I Did Wrong and How To Avoid That

MINDFULNESS DAILY JOURNAL

 ## JOURNAL

goal

MINDFULNESS DAILY JOURNAL

Date: ____/____/20__

Sun ○ Mon ○ Tue ○ Wed ○ Thu ○ Fri ○ Sat ○

IDEAS

MY MOOD TODAY
😊 ☹️ 😟 😄 😠

Today Will Be A Good Day

Meditation

How long? ____/____

How was it?   Hard ○   Easy ○

Exercise ○   Yoga/Walking/Gym/Other _____

Today I Choose to Feel
_____
_____
_____

Today I Will Focus on
_____
_____
_____

Today I feel Inspired By
_____
_____
_____

Good Habits of The Day
_____
_____
_____

To Do List
○ _____
○ _____
○ _____
○ _____

Today I'm Grateful for

MINDFULNESS DAILY JOURNAL

MY DAY

10 MINUTES TO REFLECT ON YOUR DAY

 3 Moments You'd Like To Remember

One Idea of Today That You'd Like To Explore Further

One of The Day's Challenges Big or Small

What I Did Wrong and How To Avoid That

MINDFULNESS DAILY JOURNAL

 JOURNAL

goal

MINDFULNESS DAILY JOURNAL

Date: ____/____/20__

Sun Mon Tue Wed Thu Fri Sat

IDEAS

MY MOOD TODAY

Today WILL BE A Good Day

Meditation

How long? ____/____

How was it? Hard ◯ Easy ◯

Excercise ◯   Yoga/Walking/Gym/Other _____

Today I Choose to Feel
_____
_____
_____

Today I Will Focus on
_____
_____
_____

Today I feel Inspired By
_____
_____
_____

Good Habits of The Day
_____
_____
_____

To Do List
- _____
- _____
- _____
- _____
- _____

Today I'm Grateful for

MINDFULNESS DAILY JOURNAL

MY DAY

10 MINUTES TO REFLECT ON YOUR DAY

3 Moments You'd Like To Remember

One Idea of Today That You'd Like To Explore Further

One of The Day's Challenges Big or Small

What I Did Wrong and How To Avoid That

MINDFULNESS DAILY JOURNAL

 ## JOURNAL

goal

MINDFULNESS DAILY JOURNAL

Date: ____/____/20__

Sun ○ Mon ○ Tue ○ Wed ○ Thu ○ Fri ○ Sat ○

IDEAS

MY MOOD TODAY
🙂 🙁 ☹️ 😄 😠

Today will be a Good Day

Meditation

How long? ____/____

How was it? Hard ○ Easy ○

Exercise ○   Yoga/Walking/Gym/Other _____

Today I Choose to Feel
_____
_____
_____

Today I Will Focus on
_____
_____
_____

Today I feel Inspired By
_____
_____
_____

Good Habits of The Day
_____
_____
_____

To Do List
☐ _____
☐ _____
☐ _____
☐ _____
☐ _____

Today I'm Grateful for

MINDFULNESS DAILY JOURNAL

MY DAY

10 MINUTES TO REFLECT ON YOUR DAY

3 Moments You'd Like To Remember

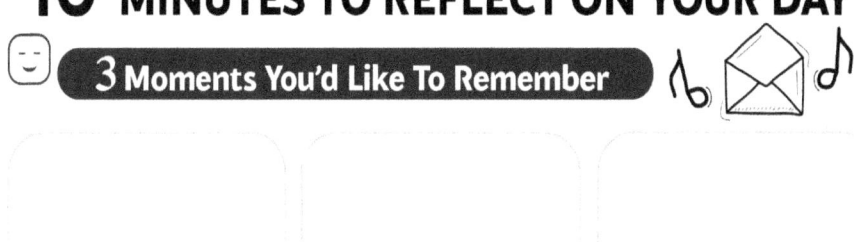

One Idea of Today That You'd Like To Explore Further

One of The Day's Challenges Big or Small

What I Did Wrong and How To Avoid That

MINDFULNESS DAILY JOURNAL

 ## JOURNAL

goal

MINDFULNESS DAILY JOURNAL

JOURNAL

goal

Hey there!!!

We hope you enjoyed our book. As a small family company, your feedback is very important to us. Please let us know how you like our book at:

believepublisher@gmail.com

Without your voice we don't exist!

Please, support us and leave a review!

Thank you!!!

www.ingramcontent.com/pod-product-compliance
Lightning Source LLC
LaVergne TN
LVHW012000070526
838202LV00054B/4990